Introductio

Using rickrack for home accessories is a unique way to use your crochet ability and give your home individual style.

Create the C
dinner time entertaining. Add an edging to bathroom hand towels and a window valance to transform the ordinary into extraordinary. You'll enjoy choosing projects in the colors that fit your own decor.

General Directions

Before you begin

Before beginning to work, remove your rickrack from the cardboard it is packaged with, put it in a mesh lingerie bag and send it through the washer. This ensures that any bleeding and shrinking will occur before you do your crochet work, and not after you've attached it to your project. Frayed ends can be trimmed and treated with liquid seam sealant, such as Fray Check.

Joining Thread to Rickrack

Rickrack has a series of tips (peaks) and valleys, Photo A.

The pattern will tell you whether to begin in a tip or valley. At first, it will take a little effort to push the crochet hook through the rickrack fabric. Be sure to keep your finger away from the point of the hook. Wearing a thimble on a finger beneath can protect it. You may want to try using an awl to put holes in the rickrack before using a hook.

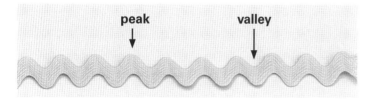

Photo A

Whichever method you use to get your hook through the rickrack, do it very near the edge. In most patterns, you will want to keep the hole centered in the tip or valley (Photo B). You may want to practice this on a scrap piece of rickrack before you start your project. Just like most skills, it will become easier to do with practice.

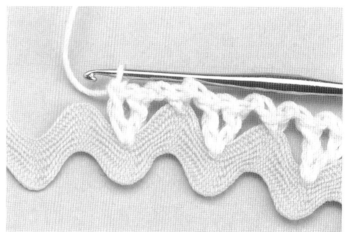

Photo B

Entwined Rickrack

For an interesting variation, two pieces of rickrack can be entwined or twisted together before adding crochet. Wrap the first couple of tips and valleys together and pin to ironing board. Continue twisting lengths together and gently press them as you go with a steam iron. Keep twisting and pressing every few inches, moving pin down as you go.

Candle Jar Edging

Design by
Maggie Petsch

INTERMEDIATE

Size

About 1¼ x 10½ inches

Materials

Size 10 crochet cotton, red (A) and mint green (B)
Medium rickrack, 1 pkg, white
Note: *Our photographed edging was made with J. & P. Coats Knit-Cro-Sheen, Spanish red #126 and mint green #28; Wrights medium rickrack, white #030.*
Size 7 (1.65mm) steel crochet hook or size needed to obtain gauge
Liquid seam sealant, such as Dritz Fray Check
Purchased candle jar
Sewing needle and matching threads

Gauge

10 sc = 1 inch

Pattern Stitch

Cluster (cl)

Keeping last lp of each tr on hook, 4 tr in st indicated, yo and draw through all 5 lps on hook.

Instructions

Note: *Please read General Directions on page 1.*

Edging

Note: *Pattern is written for 10½-inch edging. If longer or shorter edging is desired, add or subtract 2 rickrack tips for each ½ inch.*

Join B in first tip 2 inches from one end of rickrack.

Note: *For **dc dec,** yo, draw up lp in side of rickrack between tip and valley, yo, draw through 2 lps on hook; yo, draw up lp in side of rickrack between valley and next tip, yo, draw through 2 lps on hook; yo and draw through all 3 lps on hook.*

Row 1 (RS): Ch 1, sc in same tip; *ch 3, in next tip work [tr, ch 2] 3 times; tr in same tip; ch 3, sc in next tip, ch 2, **dc dec** (see Note) between last tip and next tip; ch 2, sc in next tip; rep from * 6 times more. Fasten off.

Note: *Cut rickrack about 2 inches from last tip worked.*

Hold piece with RS facing you; join A in first tr.

Row 2: Ch 3, keeping last lp of each tr on hook, 3 tr in same tr as joining; yo and draw through all 4 lps on hook—beg cl made; ch 3, [**cl** (see Pattern Stitch) in next tr, ch 3] 3 times; *cl in each of next 2 sc**, ch 3, [cl in next tr, ch 3] 4 times; rep from * 4 times more; cl in each of next 2 sc, ch 3. Fasten off, leaving an 8-inch end for sewing.

Weave in other ends.

Heading

Hold piece with RS facing you and unworked edge of rickrack at top; join B in first tip on unworked edge to right of first tip worked on opposite side; ch 1, sc in same tip; *ch 1, dc dec, ch 1, sc in next tip; rep from * 20 times more. Fasten off, leaving an 8-inch end for sewing.

Weave in other end.

Finishing

Step 1: On each end of rickrack, sk next tip after last tip worked; cut rickrack between skipped tip and next tip. Apply liquid seam sealant to edge of each cut end. Let dry.

Step 2: Fold one cut end to WS at first tip, then again to WS at last tip worked. With sewing needle and matching thread, tack folded edge to WS of rickrack. Rep with rem edge. Lightly steam press edging on WS.

Step 3: Place piece around neck of jar. With long ends left for sewing, tack ends of edging and heading tog.

Twined Scallops Edging

Design by
Maggie Petsch

INTERMEDIATE

Size
About 2 x 15½ inches

Materials
Size 10 crochet cotton, white
Chenille rickrack, 1 pkg, lavender
Note: *Our photographed edging was made with J. & P. Coats Knit-Cro-Sheen, white #001; Wrights chenille rickrack, lavender #051.*
Size 7 (1.65mm) steel crochet hook or size needed to obtain gauge
Liquid seam sealant, such as Dritz Fray Check
Purchased purple hand towel
Sewing needle and matching threads

Gauge
8 sc = 1 inch

Pattern Stitch

Quintuple treble (qntr)
Yo 6 times, insert hook in st indicated, yo, draw up lp, [yo, draw through 2 lps on hook] 7 times.

Instructions

Note: *Please read General Directions on page 1.*

Edging

Note: *Pattern is written for 15½-inch edging. If longer or shorter edging is desired, add or subtract two rickrack tips for each 1½ inches.*

Join in first tip 2 inches from one end of rickrack.

Row 1 (WS): Ch 15 (counts as a qntr and a ch-7 sp), sk next tip, sc in next tip, [ch 15, sk next tip, sc in next tip] 10 times, ch 7, **qntr** *(see Pattern Stitch)* in next tip, turn.

Note: *Cut rickrack about 2 inches from last tip worked.*

Row 2 (RS): Sl st in next ch-7 sp, ch 3 *(counts as a dc)*, 6 dc in same sp; 15 dc in each of next 10 ch-15 sps; 6 dc in next ch-15 sp; dc in 8th ch of same ch-15 sp, turn.

Row 3: Ch 3, sk first 2 dc, sl st in next dc, ch 3, sk next dc, sl st in next dc, ch 3, *****sk next dc, insert hook in next dc, yo, draw up lp, insert hook in first dc of next 15-dc group, yo, draw through dc and through 2 lps on hook; [ch 3, sk next dc, sl st in next dc] 6 times; ch 3; rep from ***** 8 times more; sk next dc, insert hook in next dc, yo, draw up lp, insert hook in first dc of next 7-dc group, yo, draw through dc and through 2 lps on hook; [ch 3, sk next dc, sl st in next dc] twice; ch 3, sl st in 3rd ch of turning ch-3. Fasten off.

Hold piece with WS facing you; join in same tip as first sc of Row 1 made.

Row 4: Ch 1, sc in same tip; *****ch 17, working in front of next ch-15 sp of Row 1, sc in next unused tip, ch 17; working behind next ch-15 sp, sc in next unused tip; rep from ***** 4 times more; ch 17, working in front of next ch-7 sp, sc in same tip as last sc of Row 1 made, turn.

Row 5: Ch 1, sl st in next ch-17 sp, ch 4 *(counts as a tr)*, 16 tr in same sp; 17 tr in each rem ch-17 sp, turn.

Row 6: Ch 3, sk first 2 tr, sl st in next tr, [ch 3, sk next tr, sl st in next tr] twice, *****ch 3, sk next tr, in next tr work (sl st, ch 5, sl st); [ch 3, sk next tr, sl st in next tr] 3 times, ch 3, sk next tr, insert hook in next tr, yo, draw up lp, insert hook in first tr of next 17-tr group, yo, draw through tr and through 2 lps on hook; [ch 3, sk next tr, st sl in next tr] 3 times; rep from ***** 9 times more; ch 3, sk next tr, in next tr work (sl st, ch 5, sl st); [ch 3, sk next tr, sl st in next tr] 3 times, ch 3, sk next tr, sl st in 4th ch of beg ch-4 of previous row.

Fasten off.

Heading

Hold piece with WS facing you and unworked edge of rickrack at top; join in tip opposite valley between first two worked tips on edging edge.

Row 1 (RS): Ch 1, sc in same tip; [ch 6, sc in next tip] 21 times, turn.

Row 2: Ch 1, sc in first sc, ch 2, sl st in sc just made—picot made; *6 sc in next ch-6 sp; sc in next sc, picot; rep from * across.

Fasten off and weave in all ends.

Finishing

Step 1: On each end of rickrack, sk next tip after last tip worked; cut rickrack between skipped tip and next tip. Apply liquid seam sealant to edge of each cut end. Let dry.

Step 2: Fold one cut end to WS at first tip then again to WS at last tip worked. With sewing needle and matching thread, tack folded edge to WS of rickrack. Rep with rem edge. Lightly steam press crocheted portion of trim only on WS.

Step 3: With sewing needle and matching thread, tack heading to towel.

Holiday Edging

Design by
Maggie Petsch

INTERMEDIATE

Size

Place Mat: 13 x 18 inches
Napkin Ring: 1½ inches wide

Materials

Size 10 crochet cotton, red
Medium rickrack, 2 pkgs, green *(A)*
Medium metallic rickrack, 2 pkgs, multicolored (B)
Note: *Our photographed edgings were made with J. & P. Coats Knit-Cro-Sheen, Spanish red #126; Wrights medium rickrack, emerald #044; Wrights medium metallic rickrack, multi #001.*
Size 7 (1.65mm) steel crochet hook or size needed to obtain gauge
Liquid seam sealant, such as Dritz Fray Check
Purchased place mat
Sewing needle and matching thread

Gauge

10 sc = 1 inch

Pattern Stitch

Cluster (cl)
Keeping last lp of each dc on hook, 3 dc in st indicated, yo and draw through all 4 lps on hook.

Instructions

Note: Please read General Directions on page 1.

Place Mat

Note: Pattern is worked for an edging to fit a 12 x 18-inch place mat.

Horizontal Strip (make 2)

Note: Beg about 2 inches from end of rickrack, twist A and B rickracks tog for 20 inches. Cut rickrack about 2 inches from last twist.

Heading

Note: Heading is worked on RS.

Join in first B tip; ch 1, sc in same tip; *ch 4, sc in next B tip; rep from * 36 times more. Fasten off.

Edging

Hold piece with RS facing you and unworked edge of strip at top; join in first A tip directly above first sc on opposite edge of rickrack.

Row 1 (RS): Ch 1, sc in same tip; *ch 4, sc in next A tip; rep from * 36 times more; turn.

Row 2: Sl st in next ch-4 sp, ch 2, keeping last lp of each dc on hook, 2 dc in same sp; yo and draw through all 3 lps on hook—beg cl made; *ch 2, in next ch-4 sp work [**cl** *(see Pattern Stitch),* ch 3, cl]—shell made; rep from * 36 times more; turn.

Row 3: Sl st in next cl and in next ch-3 sp, ch 1, sc in same sp, ch 3, sl st in sc just made—picot made; *ch 2, sc in next ch-2 sp, ch 2, sc in ch-3 sp of next shell sp, ch 3, sl st in sc just made—picot made; rep from * across.

Fasten off and weave in ends.

Vertical Strip (make 2)

Note: Beg about 2 inches from end of rickrack, twist A and B rickracks tog for 15 inches. Cut rickrack about 2 inches from last twist.

Heading

Note: Heading is worked on RS.

Join red in first B tip, ch 1, sc in same tip; *ch 4, sc in next B tip; rep from * 26 times more. Fasten off.

Edging

Hold piece with RS facing you; join red in first A rickrack tip directly above first sc on opposite edge of rickrack.

Row 1 (RS): Ch 1, sc in same tip; *ch 4, sc in next A tip; rep from * 26 times more; turn.

Row 2: Sl st in next ch-4 sp, beg cl in same sp; *ch 2, shell in next ch-4 sp; rep from * across; turn.

Row 3: Sl st in next cl and in next ch-3 sp, ch 1, sc in same sp, ch 3, sl st in sc just made—picot made; *ch 2, sc in next ch-2 sp, ch 2, sc in ch-3 sp of next shell sp, ch 3, sl st in sc just made—picot made; rep from * across.

Fasten off and weave in all ends.

Napkin Ring

Note: Beg about 2 inches from end of rickrack, twist A and B rickracks tog for 14 inches. Cut rickrack about 2 inches from last twist.

First Side

Join in first B tip.

Row 1 (RS): Ch 1, sc in same tip; *ch 4, sc in next B tip; rep from * 14 times more; turn.

Row 2: Sl st in next ch-4 sp, beg cl in same sp; *ch 2, shell in next ch-4 sp; rep from * across, turn.

Row 3: Sl st in next cl and in next ch-3 sp, ch 1, sc in same sp, ch 3, sl st in sc just made—picot made; *ch 2, sc in next ch-2 sp, ch 2, sc in ch-3 sp of next shell sp, ch 3, sl st in sc just made—picot made; rep from * across.

Fasten off.

Second Side

Hold piece with RS facing you and unworked edge of strip at top; join in first A tip directly above first sc on opposite edge of rickrack.

Row 1 (RS): Ch 1, sc in same tip, *ch 4, sc in next A tip; rep from * 26 times more; turn.

Rows 2 & 3: Rep Rows 2 and 3 of First Side.

Finishing

Step 1: On each end of rickrack, sk next tip after last tip worked; cut rickrack between skipped tip and next tip. Apply liquid seam sealant to edge of each cut end. Let dry.

Step 2: Fold one cut end to WS at first tip, then again to WS at last tip worked. With sewing needle and matching thread, tack folded edge to WS of rickrack. Rep with rem ends. Lightly steam press crocheted portion of trim only on WS.

Step 3: For place mat, lay one horizontal strip across top of placemat and one across bottom. Lay one vertical strip down each side. Beg at bottom left corner, place end of vertical strip over end of horizontal strip; at bottom right corner, place end of horizontal strip over end of vertical strip; at top right corner, place end of vertical strip over end of horizontal strip; at upper left corner, place end of horizontal strip over end of vertical strip. With sewing needle and matching thread, tack edgings to place mat across heading side.

Step 4: For napkin ring, sew ends of rickrack strip tog on WS. On each side, tack ends of crocheted edging tog. Turn RS out.

Pleasing Pineapples Edging

Design by
Maggie Petsch

INTERMEDIATE

Size

About 2 x 15½ inches

Materials

Size 10 crochet cotton, white
Chenille rickrack, 1 pkg, yellow
Note: *Our photographed edging was made with J. & P. Coats Knit-Cro-Sheen, white #001; Wrights chenille rickrack, lemon ice #012.*
Size 7 (1.65mm) steel crochet hook
   or size needed to obtain gauge
Liquid seam sealant, such as Dritz
   Fray Check
Purchased yellow hand towel
Sewing needle and matching threads

Gauge

10 sc = 1 inch

Pattern Stitch

Shell
In st indicated work (2 dc, ch 2, 2 dc).

Instructions

Note: *Please read General Directions on page 1.*

Edging

Note: *Pattern is written for 15½-inch edging. If longer or shorter edging is desired, add or subtract two rickrack tips for each 1½ inches.*

Join in first tip 2 inches from one end of rickrack.

Row 1 (RS): Ch 3 *(counts as a dc)*, in same tip work (dc, ch 2, 2 dc)—beg shell made; *ch 4, in next tip work (dc, ch 2, dc)—V-st made; ch 4, **shell** *(see Pattern Stitch)* in next tip; rep from * 9 times more, turn.

Note: *Cut rickrack about 2 inches from last tip worked.*

Row 2: Ch 4 *(counts as a tr)*, shell in next ch-2 sp; *ch 3, 5 dc in ch-2 sp of next V-st—base of pineapple made; ch 3, shell in next ch-2 sp; rep * 9 times more; tr in 3rd ch of beg ch-3, turn.

Row 3: Ch 4, shell in next shell; *ch 1, dc in first dc of next 5-dc group, ch 1, [dc in next dc, ch 1] 5 times; shell in next shell; rep from * 9 times more; tr in turning ch-4 sp, turn.

Row 4: Ch 4, shell in next shell; *ch 3, sk next ch-1 sp, [sc in next ch-1 sp, ch 3] 4 times; shell in next shell; rep from * 9 times more; tr in turning ch-4 sp, turn.

Row 5: Ch 4, shell in next shell; *ch 3, sk next ch-3 sp, [sc in next ch-3 sp, ch 3] 3 times; in next ch-2 sp work (shell, ch 2, 2 dc); rep from * 8 times more; ch 3, sk next ch-3 sp, [sc in next ch-3 sp, ch 3] 3 times; shell in next shell; tr in turning ch-4 sp, turn.

First Pineapple

Row 6: Ch 4, shell in next shell; ch 3, sk next ch-3 sp, [sc in next ch-3 sp, ch 3] twice; shell in next ch-2 sp; tr in next dc, turn, leaving rem sts unworked.

Row 7: Ch 4, shell in next shell; ch 3, sk next ch-3 sp, sc in next ch-3 sp, ch 3, shell in next shell; tr in turning ch-4 sp, turn.

Row 8: Ch 4, [shell in next shell] twice; tr in turning ch-4 sp, turn.

Row 9: Ch 3, keeping last lp of each dc on hook, 2 dc in each of next 2 ch-2 sps; tr in turning ch-4 sp, yo and draw through all 6 lps on hook. Fasten off.

Second Pineapple

Hold piece with RS facing you; join in next unused dc on shell on Row 5.

Row 1: Ch 4, shell in next ch-2 sp, ch 3, sk next ch-3 sp, [sc in next ch-3 sp, ch 3] twice; shell in next ch-2 sp; tr in next dc, turn.

Rows 2–4: Rep Rows 7–9 of first pineapple.

Third–Ninth Pineapples

Work same as Second Pineapple.

Tenth Pineapple

Hold piece with RS facing you; join in next unused dc on shell on Row 5.

Row 1: Ch 4, shell in next ch-2 sp; ch 3, sk next ch-3 sp, [sc in next ch-3 sp, ch 3] twice; shell in next shell; tr in turning ch-4 sp, turn.

Rows 2–4: Rep Rows 2–4 of Second Pineapple.

Border

Hold piece with RS facing you; join in 3rd ch of beg ch-3 of Row 1; [ch 3, sl st in sp formed by end st of next row] 8 times; *ch 3, in tip of next pineapple work (sl st, ch 5, sl st); ch 3, sl st in sp formed by end st of Row 9; [ch 3, sl st in sp formed by end st of next row] twice; ch 3, insert hook in sp formed by end st of next row, yo, draw up lp, insert hook in sp formed by end st of corresponding row on next pineapple, yo, draw through sp and through 2 lps on hook; [ch 3, sl st in sp formed by end st of next row] 3 times; rep from * 8 times more; ch 3, in tip of next pineapple work (sl st, ch 5, sl st); ch 3, sl st sp formed by end st of Row 9; [ch 3, sl st in sp formed by end st of next row] 8 times.

Fasten off.

Heading

Hold piece with RS facing you and unworked edge of rickrack at top; join in tip opposite valley between first two worked tips on edging edge.

Row 1 (RS): Ch 1, sc in same tip; *ch 6, sc in next tip; rep from * across, turn.

Row 2: Ch 5, sl st in first sc, *ch 3, sk next 2 chs, sl st in next ch, ch 3, sl st in next ch, ch 3, sk next 2 chs, in next sc work (sl st, ch 5, sl st); rep from * across.

Fasten off and weave in all ends.

Finishing

Step 1: On each end of rickrack, sk next tip after last tip worked; cut rickrack between skipped tip and next tip. Apply liquid seam sealant to edge of each cut end. Let dry.

Step 2: Fold one cut end to WS at first tip, then again to WS at last tip worked. With sewing needle and matching thread, tack folded edge to WS of rickrack. Rep with rem side. Lightly steam press crocheted portion of trim only on WS.

Step 3: With sewing needle and matching thread, tack heading to towel.

Multi-Tier Edging

Design by
Sandi Marshall

INTERMEDIATE

Size

About 3⅛ inches at widest point x
  desired length

Materials

Size 10 crochet cotton, beige
Jumbo rickrack, black
Note: *Our photographed edging was made with Coats & Clark South Maid, camel #433; Wrights jumbo rickrack, black #031.*
Size 8 (1.5mm) steel crochet hook
  or size needed to obtain gauge
Liquid seam sealant, such as Dritz
  Fray Check
Purchased valance
Sewing needle and matching
  threads

Gauge

11 sc = 1 inch

Pattern Stitch

Puff Stitch (puff st)

[Yo, insert hook in st indicated, yo, draw through] 4 times; yo and draw through all 9 lps on hook; ch 1.

Instructions

Note: Please read General Directions on page 1.

Edging

Heading

Note: Cut two pieces of rickrack 4 inches longer than desired length of edging.

Join in right-hand edge of first tip 2 inches from end of one rickrack piece.

Row 1 (WS): Ch 3 *(counts as a dc on this and following rows)*, 2 dc evenly spaced in same tip; *ch 4, sc in next valley, ch 4, 3 dc *(evenly spaced)* across next tip; rep from * to about 2 inches from end of rickrack, turn.

Row 2 (RS): Ch 4 *(counts as a dc and a ch-1 sp)*, dc in first dc, **puff st** *(see Pattern Stitch)* in next dc; in next dc work (dc, ch 1, dc)—V-st made; *ch 2, sk next sc, V-st in next dc; puff st in next dc; V-st in next dc; rep from * to last sc; ch 2, sk last sc, V-st in next dc; puff st in next dc; V-st in 3rd ch of beg ch-3, turn.

Row 3: Ch 3; *V-st in next ch-1 sp; ch 1, sk next puff st, V-st in ch-1 sp of next V-st; 2 dc in next ch-2 sp; rep from * to last 2 V-sts; V-st in ch-1 sp of next V-st; ch 1, sk next puff st, V-st in ch-1 sp of last V-st; dc in 3rd ch of turning ch-4, turn.

Row 4: Ch 3; *V-st in next V-st; puff st in next ch-1 sp; V-st in next V-st; ch 1, sk next 2 dc, rep from * to last 2 V-sts; V-st in next V-st; puff st in next ch-1 sp; V-st in next V-st; dc in 3rd ch of turning ch-3, turn.

Row 5: Ch 1, sc in each dc, in each ch-1 sp and in each puff st. Fasten off.

Border

Hold piece with RS facing you and unworked edge of rickrack at top; join in valley opposite first tip worked on heading edge; ch 3, 2 dc evenly spaced in same tip; *ch 4, sc in next valley, ch 4, 3 dc *(evenly spaced)* across next tip; rep from * across.

Fasten off and set aside.

Join in right-hand edge of first tip 2 inches from end of 2nd rickrack piece.

Row 1 (RS): Ch 3, 2 dc evenly spaced in same tip; *ch 4, sc in next valley, ch 4, 3 dc *(evenly spaced)* across next tip; rep from * to about 2 inches from end of rickrack, turn.

Hold WS of border of first rickrack piece facing WS of working piece and carefully match sts.

Note: On following row, join pieces by working through corresponding sts on both pieces at same time. To keep joining flat, work in front lps only of sts on working piece and back lps only of sts on first piece.

Row 2: Ch 1, sc in first dc and in next 2 dc; *ch 5, sl st in 3rd ch from hook—picot made; ch 2, sc in next 3 dc; rep from * across. Fasten off.

Hold piece with RS facing you and unworked edge of rickrack at top; join in valley opposite first tip worked.

Row 1: Ch 3, 2 dc evenly spaced in same tip; * ch 4, sc in next valley, ch 4, 3 dc *(evenly spaced)* across next tip; rep from * across, turn.

Row 2 (RS): Ch 4 *(counts as a dc and a ch-1 sp)*, dc in first dc, puff st in next dc; V-st in next dc; *ch 2, sk next sc, V-st in next dc; puff st in next dc; V-st in next dc; rep from * to last sc; ch 2, sk last sc, V-st in next dc; puff st in next dc; V-st in 3rd ch of beg ch-3, turn.

Row 3: Ch 3; *V-st in next ch-1 sp; ch 1, sk next puff st, V-st in ch-1 sp of next V-st; 2 dc in next ch-2 sp; rep from * to last 2 V-sts; V-st in ch-1 sp of next V-st; ch 1, sk next puff st, V-st in ch-1 sp of last V-st; dc in 3rd ch of turning ch-4, turn.

Row 4: Ch 1, sc in first dc, sk next V-st, *in next ch-1 sp work (V-st, ch 2, tr, ch 2, V-st); ch 1, sk next V-st, sc in next 2 dc; rep from * to last ch-1 sp; in last ch-1 sp work (V-st, ch 2, tr, ch 2, V-st); ch 1, sc in 3rd ch of turning ch-3.

Fasten off and weave in all ends.

Finishing

Step 1: On each end of rickrack, sk next tip after last tip worked; cut rickrack between skipped tip and next tip. Apply liquid seam sealant to edge of each cut end. Let dry.

Step 2: Fold one cut end to WS at first tip then again to WS at last tip worked. With sewing needle and matching thread, tack folded edge to WS of rickrack. Rep with rem edges. Lightly steam press crocheted portion of trim only on WS.

Step 3: With sewing needle and matching thread, sew heading to valance.

Flowering Table Runner

Design by
Maggie Petsch

INTERMEDIATE

Size
About 12 x 42 inches

Materials
Size 10 crochet cotton, 675 yds
white *(A)*; 150 yds each, purple
(B), rose *(C)* and blue *(D)*
Medium rickrack, 4 pkgs green
Note: *Our photographed edging
was made with J. & P. Coats Knit-
Cro-Sheen, white #001, lilac #36,
mid rose #46A and crystal blue #25;
Wrights medium rickrack, emerald
#044.*
Size 7 (1.65mm) steel crochet hook or size needed to
obtain gauge
Liquid seam sealant, such as Dritz Fray Check
Sewing needle and matching thread

Gauge
Rnds 1–5 = 1⅜ inch

Instructions
Note: *Please read General Directions on page 1.*

Rickrack Circle (make 52)

Cut 52 pieces of rickrack, each having 14 full tips.
Apply liquid seam sealant to each cut end. Let dry. On
each end, fold rickrack to WS at first tip, then again at
next valley to form half-tip. With sewing needle and
matching thread, tack fold to WS. Bring half-tip at
each end tog to form circle with 12 tips and sew seam
securely on WS at folded edge.

Motifs

Motif A (make 22)
With A, ch 3.

Rnd 1 (RS): 11 hdc in 3rd ch from hook (beg 2 skipped
chs count as a hdc); join in 2nd ch of beg 2 skipped chs.
(12 hdc)

Rnd 2: Ch 1, sc in same ch as joining, ch 3, sk next hdc,
[sc in next hdc, ch 3, sk next hdc] 5 times; join in first sc.
Fasten off. *(6 ch-3 sps)*

Hold piece with RS facing you; join B in any ch-3 sp.

Rnd 3: Ch 1, in same sp and in each rem ch-3 sp work
(sc, 5 dc, sc)—petal made. Do not join. *(6 petals)*

Rnd 4: Working behind petals made in last rnd, sc in
first skipped sc of Rnd 2, ch 4, [sc in next skipped sc,
ch 4] 5 times; join in first sc. *(6 ch-4 sps)*

Rnd 5: Sl st in next ch-4 sp, ch 1, in same sp and in
each rem ch-4 sp work (sc, 7 dc, sc)—large petal made.
Do not join. *(6 large petals)*

Rnd 6: Working behind petals made in last rnd, sl st in
first unworked sc of Rnd 4, ch 6, [sl st in next unworked
sc of Rnd 6, ch 6] 5 times; join in first sl st. Fasten off. *(6
ch-6 sps)*

Hold piece with RS facing you; join A in 2nd ch of any
ch-6 sp.

Rnd 7: Ch 3, sl st in seam at tip on inner edge of rickrack
circle; *****ch 3, sk next 2 chs of same ch-6 sp, sl st in next
ch, ch 3, sl st in next tip on inner edge of rickrack circle,
ch 3, sl st in 2nd ch of next ch-6 sp, ch 3, sl st in next tip
on rickrack circle; rep from ***** 4 times more; ch 3, sk next
2 chs on same ch-6 sp, sl st in next ch, ch 3, sl st in next
tip on inner edge of rickrack circle, ch 3; join in first ch of
beg ch-3.

Fasten off and weave in ends.

Motif B (make 15)
With A, ch 3.

Rnds 1 & 2: Rep Rnds 1 and 2.

Rnds 3–6: With C, rep Rnds 3–6 of Motif A.

Rnd 7: Rep Rnd 7.

Motif C (make 15)

With A, ch 3.

Rnds 1 & 2: Rep Rnds 1 and 2 of Motif A.

Rnds 3–6: With D, rep Rnds 3–6 of Motif A.

Rnd 7: Rep Rnd 7 of Motif A.

Center Panel

For Center Panel, join Motif A's in 2 rows of 11 motifs each. Join motifs as follows.

First Motif

Hold one Motif A with RS facing you; join A in any tip on outer edge of rickrack circle.

Rnd 1: Ch 9; *sl st in next tip, ch 9; rep from * 10 times more; join in joining sl st. *(12 ch-9 sps)*

Rnd 2: Sl st in next ch-9 sp, ch 1, in same sp and in each rem ch-9 sp work (4 sc, ch 3, sc, ch 5, sc, ch 3, 4 sc); join in first sc.

Fasten off and weave in ends.

Second Motif

Hold 2nd Motif A with RS facing you; join A in any tip on outer edge of rickrack circle.

Rnd 1: Ch 9; *sl st in next tip, ch 9; rep from * 10 times more; join in joining sl st. *(12 ch-9 sps)*

Rnd 2: Sl st in next ch-9 sp, ch 1, in same sp and in next 8 ch-9 sps work (4 sc, ch 3, sc, ch 5, sc, ch 3, 4 sc); in next ch-9 sp work (4 sc, ch 3, sc, ch 2); hold WS of completed motif facing WS of working motif and carefully match sts; *on completed motif, sl st in corresponding ch-5 sp, ch 2; on working motif, in same ch-9 sp work (sc, ch 3, 4 sc); in next ch-9 sp work (4 sc, ch 3, ch 2); rep from * twice more; join in first sc.

Fasten off and weave in ends.

Join remaining Motif A's in same manner.

Border

Alternating Motifs B and C, join motifs around outer edge of center panel in same manner.

Colorful Doily & Coaster

Design by
Sandi Marshall

EXPERIENCED

Size

Doily: About 16 inches in diameter
Coaster: About 4 inches in diameter

Materials

Size 10 crochet cotton, beige *(A)*, dk green *(B)* and variegated *(C)*
Jumbo printed rickrack, 1 pkg, variegated
Note: *Our photographed set was made with Coats & Clark South Maid, new ecru #429, forest green #449 and ocean #995; Wrights jumbo printed rickrack, rainbow #001.*
Size 8 (1.50mm) steel crochet hook or size needed to obtain gauge
Liquid seam sealant, such as Dritz Fray Check
Sewing needle and matching thread

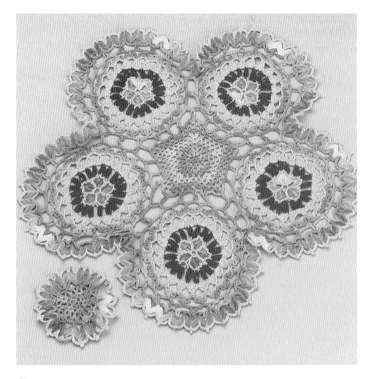

Gauge

11 sc = 1 inch

Pattern Stitches

Triple treble (trtr)
Yo 4 times, insert hook in st indicated, yo, draw lp through, (yo, draw through 2 lps on hook) 5 times.

Cluster (cl)
Keeping last lp of each trtr on hook, 3 trtr in st indicated; yo and draw through all 4 lps on hook.

Treble Cluster (tr cl)
Keeping last lp of each tr on hook, 3 tr in st indicated; yo and draw through all 4 lps on hook.

Double Treble (dtr)
Yo 3 times, insert hook in st indicated, yo, draw lp through, (yo, draw through 2 lps on hook) 4 times.

Shell
In sp indicated work (2 dc, ch 3, 2 dc).

Instructions

Note: Please read General Directions on page 1.

Motif A

Join A in first tip 2 inches from one end of rickrack.

Inner Rnd: Ch 1, sc in same tip; ch 2; *sc in next tip, ch 2; rep from * 4 times more; join in first sc. Remove hook.

Apply liquid seam sealant to each cut end. Let dry. On each end, fold rickrack to WS at first tip, then again at next valley to form half-tip. With sewing needle and matching thread, tack fold to WS. Bring half-tip at each end tog to form circle with five tips and sew seam securely on WS at folded edge.

Hold piece with unworked edge of rickrack at top; reinsert hook in lp left at end of Inner Rnd.

Rnd 1 (RS): Ch 4, working on unworked edge, sc in valley directly above last worked tip, tr in sc on Inner Rnd at base of beg ch-4; *ch 3, sc in side of rickrack between valley and next tip, ch 4, 3 sc evenly spaced in next tip; ch 4, sc in side of rickrack between tip and next valley, ch 3, sc in next valley, ch 4, sl st in sc directly below on Inner Rnd, ch 4, sc in same valley beside last sc; rep from * 3 times more; ch 3, sc in side of rickrack between valley and next tip, ch 4, 3 sc evenly spaced in next tip; ch 4, sc in side of rickrack between tip and next valley, ch 3, sc in next valley; join in first sc.

Note: On following rnd, sl st around back threads only of post (see Stitch Guide on page 15) of sc.

Rnd 2: Sl st in next tr; *ch 5, sk next sc, working in back of piece (see Note), sl st around post of next sc, ch 4, sk next sc, sl st around post of next sc, ch 5, sk next sc, sl st in next 2 sc; rep from * 3 times more; ch 5, sk next sc, working in back of piece, sl st around post of next sc, ch 4, sk next sc, sl st around post of next sc, ch 5, sk next sc, join in joning sl st. Fasten off.

Hold piece with RS facing you; join B in ch-5 sp to right of any tip.

Rnd 3: Ch 5 *(counts as first trtr)*, keeping last lp of each trtr on hook, 2 **trtr** *(see Pattern Stitches)* in same sp; yo and draw through all 3 lps on hook—beg cl made; ch 4, in next ch-4 sp work **tr cl** *(see Pattern Stitches)*; ch 4, in next ch-5 sp work [**cl** *(see Pattern Stitches)*, ch 4, cl); ch 4; *in next ch-5 sp work cl; ch 4, in next ch-4 sp work tr cl; ch 4, in next ch-5 sp work (cl, ch 4, cl); ch 4; rep from * 3 times more; join in beg cl. Fasten off.

Hold piece with RS facing you; join A in any tr cl at top of any tip.

Rnd 4: Ch 3 (counts as a hdc and a ch-1 sp); *in next ch-4 sp work [dc, ch 1, tr, ch 1, **dtr** *(see Pattern Stitches)*, ch 2, dtr, ch 1, tr, ch 1, dc]; ch 1, hdc in next cluster, ch 1; rep from * 18 times more; in next ch-4 sp work (dc, ch 1, tr, ch 1, dtr), ch 2, dtr, ch 1, tr, ch 1, dc); ch 1; join in 2nd ch of beg ch-3.

Rnd 5: Sl st in each st and in each ch-1 sp to next ch-2 sp and in next ch-2 sp; ch 1, sc in same sp; ch 6; *sc in ch-2 sp, ch 6; rep from * 19 times more; join in first sc.

Rnd 6: Ch 1, sc in same sc; 7 sc in next ch-6 sp; sc in next sc, 7 sc in next ch-6 sp; rep from * 19 times more; join in first sc. Change to C; cut A.

Rnd 7: Ch 1, *sc in next sc, sk next 2 sc, in next sc work (dc, ch 3, dc, ch 1, dc, ch 1, dc, ch 3, dc); sk next 2 sc, sc in next sc, sl st in next sc; rep from * 18 times more; sc in next sc, sk next 2 sc, in next sc work (dc, ch 3, dc, ch 1, dc, ch 1, dc, ch 3, dc); sk next 2 sc, sc in next sc; join in first sc.

Rnd 8: Sl st in next dc, in next 3 chs, in next dc, in next ch and in next dc; ch 1, sc in same dc; ch 7; *sc in 3rd dc on next 5-dc group, ch 7; rep from * 18 times more; join in first sc.

Rnd 9: Sl st in next ch-7 sp; in same sp and in each rem ch-7 sp work (4 sc, ch 8, 4 sc); join in first sc. Fasten off.

Motif B

Work same as Motif A through Rnd 8.

Rnd 9: Sl st in next ch-7 sp; in same sp and in next 16 ch-7 sps work (4 sc, ch 8, 4 sc); 4 sc in next ch-7 sp; ch 4; hold WS of completed motif facing WS of working motif and carefully match sts; on completed motif, sl st in corresponding ch-8 sp, ch 4; on working motif, 4 sc in same ch-7 sp; [4 sc in next ch-7 sp; ch 4; on completed motif, sl st in next ch-8 sp, ch 4; on working motif, 4 sc in same ch-7 sp] twice; join in first sc. Mark first joined sp and 4th ch-8 sp on Motif B to right of same sp. On Motif A, mark 6th ch-8 sp to left of first joined sp. Fasten off.

Motif C

Work same as Motif A through Rnd 8.

Rnd 9: Sl st in next ch-7 sp; in same sp and in next 16 ch-7 sps work (4 sc, ch 8, 4 sc); 4 sc in next ch-7 sp; ch 4; hold WS of last completed motif facing WS of working motif and carefully match sts; on completed motif, sl st in marked ch-8 sp, ch 4; on working motif, 4 sc in same ch-7 sp; [4 sc in next ch-7 sp; ch 4; on completed motif, sl st in next ch-8 sp, ch 4; on working motif, 4 sc in same ch-7 sp] twice; join in first sc. Mark first joined sp and 4th ch-8 sp on Motif C to right of same sp. Fasten off.

Motif D

Work same as Motif C, marking first joined sp and 4th ch-8 sp on Motif D to right of same sp.

Motif E

Work same as Motif A through Rnd 8.

Rnd 9: Sl st in next ch-7 sp; in same sp and in next 10 ch-7 sps work (4 sc, ch 8, 4 sc); 4 sc in next ch-7 sp; ch 4; hold WS of Motif A facing WS of working motif and carefully match sts; on Motif A, sl st in marked ch-8 sp, ch 4; on working motif, 4 sc in same ch-7 sp; [4 sc in next ch-7 sp; ch 4; on Motif A, sl st in next ch-8 sp, ch 4; on working motif, 4 sc in same ch-7 sp] twice; in each of next 3 ch-8 sps work (4 sc, ch 8, 4 sc); 4 sc in next ch-7 sp; ch 4; hold WS of Motif D facing WS of working motif and carefully match sts; on Motif D, sl st in marked ch-8 sp, ch 4; on working motif, 4 sc in same ch-7 sp; [4 sc in next ch-7 sp; ch 4; on Motif A, sl st in next ch-8 sp, ch 4; on working motif, 4 sc in same ch-7 sp] twice; join in first sc. Fasten off.

Center

With C, ch 7; join to form a ring.

Rnd 1 (RS): Ch 1, [sc in ring, ch 6] 5 times; join in first sc.

Rnd 2: Sl st in next 3 chs of next ch-6 sp; ch 3, in same sp work (dc, ch 2, 2 dc); ch 1; *in next ch-6 sp work (2 dc, ch 2, 2 dc), ch 1; rep from * 4 times more; join in 3rd ch of beg ch-3.

Rnd 3: Sl st in next dc and in next ch-2 sp, ch 3 *(counts as a dc on this and following rnds)* in same sp work (dc, ch 3, 2 dc)—beg shell made; *ch 6, sc in next ch-1 sp, ch 6, **shell** *(see Pattern Stitches)* in next ch-2 sp; rep from * 3 times more; ch 3, sc in next ch-6 sp, ch 6; join in 3rd ch of beg ch-3.

Rnd 4: Sl st in next dc and in next ch-3 sp, beg shell in same sp; *ch 4, [sc in next ch-6 sp, ch 4] twice; shell in ch-3 sp of next shell; rep from * 3 times more; ch 4, [sc in next ch-6 sp, ch 4] twice; join in 3rd ch of beg ch-3. Fasten off.

Hold piece with RS facing you; join A in ch-3 sp of any shell.

Rnd 5: Beg shell in same sp; *ch 4, [sc in next ch-6 sp, ch 4] 3 times; shell in next shell; rep from * 3 times more; ch 4, [sc in next ch-6 sp, ch 4] 3 times; join in 3rd ch of beg ch-3.

Rnd 6: Sl st in next dc and in next ch-3 sp; beg shell in same sp; *ch 4, [sc in next ch-4 sp, ch 4] 4 times; shell in next shell; rep from * 3 times more; ch 4, [sc in next ch-4 sp, ch 4] 4 times; join in 3rd ch of beg ch-3. Fasten off.

Hold piece with RS facing you; join C in ch-3 sp of any shell.

Rnd 7: Beg shell in same sp; *ch 4, [sc in next ch-4 sp, ch 4] 5 times; shell in next shell; rep from * 3 times more; ch 4, [sc in next ch-4 sp, ch 4] 5 times; join in 3rd ch of beg ch-3.

Rnd 8: Sl st in next dc and in next ch-3 sp; beg shell in same sp; *ch 4, [sc in next ch-4 sp, ch 4] 6 times; shell in next shell; rep from * 3 times more; ch 4, [sc in next ch-4 sp, ch 4] 6 times; join in 3rd ch of beg ch-3.

Note: On following rnd, center is joined to joined motifs.

Rnd 9: Ch 1, sc in same ch as joining and in next dc; sl st in next ch-3 sp, ch 6, sl st in joining of marked joined sp between any 2 motifs, ch 6, sc in next 2 dc on center, [4 sc in each of next 2 ch-4 sps; ch 2, sl st in next ch-8 sp on motif, ch 2] 3 times; 4 sc in each of next 2 ch-4 sp; *sc in next 2 dc, sl st in next ch-3 sp, ch 6, sl st in joining of next marked joined sp, ch 6, sc in next 2 dc on center, [4 sc in each of next 2 ch-4 sps; ch 2, sl st in next ch-8 sp on motif, ch 2] 3 times; 4 sc in each of next 2 ch-4 sp; rep from * 3 times more; sl st in next ch-3 sp, ch 6, sl st in joining of marked joined sp between any 2 motifs, ch 6, sc in next 2 dc on center, [4 sc in each of next 2 ch-4 sps; ch 2, sl st in next ch-8 sp on motif, ch 2] 3 times; 4 sc in each of next 2 ch-4 sp; join in first sc. Fasten off.

Outer Edging

Join C in first tip about 2 inches from end of rickrack.

Rnd 1: Ch 1, sc in same tip; *ch 6, sc in next valley, ch 6, sc in next tip; rep from * 84 times more; ch 6, sc in next valley; join in first sc.

Note: Cut rickrack about 2 inches from last worked tip.

Rnd 2: Ch 1, sc in same tip; sl st in 7th unused ch-8 sp of any motif; 5 sc in next ch-6 sp on edging; [sl st in next sc, 5 sc in each of next 2 ch-6 sps; ch 1, sl st in next ch-8 sp on motif, ch 1, 5 sc in each of next 2 ch-6 sps; sl st in next sc, 5 sc in next ch-6 sp; sl st in next ch-8 sp on motif, 5 sc in next ch-6 sp] twice; sl st in next sc, 5 sc in next ch-6 sp; sl st in next joined ch-8 sps on motifs, 5 sc in next ch-6 sp; sl st in next sc, 5 sc in next ch-6 sp; sl st in next ch-8 sp on motif, 5 sc in next ch-6 sp; [sl st in next sc, 5 sc in each of next 2 ch-6 sps; ch 1, sl st in next ch-8 sp on motif, ch 1, 5 sc in each of next 2 ch-6 sps; sl st in next sc, 5 sc in next ch-6 sp; sl st in next ch-8 sp on motif, 5 sc in next ch-6 sp] 5 times; sl st in next sc, 5 sc in next ch-6 sp, sl st in next joined ch-8 sps on motifs, 5 sc in each of next 2 ch-6 sps; sl st in next ch-8 sp on motif, 5 sc in next ch-6 sp; [sl st in next sc, 5 sc in each of next 2 ch-6 sps; ch 1, sl st in next ch-8 sp on motif, ch 1, 5 sc in each of next 2 ch-6 sps; sl st in next sc, 5 sc in next ch-6 sp; sl st in next ch-8 sp on motif, 5 sc in next ch-6 sp] 5 times; sl st in next sc, 5 sc in next ch-6 sp; sl st in next joined ch-8 sps on motifs, 5 sc in each of next 2 ch-6 sps; ch 1, sl st in next ch-8 sp on motif, ch 1, 5 sc in next ch-6 sp; [sl st in next sc, 5 sc in each of next 2 ch-6 sps; ch 1, sl st in next ch-8 sp on motif, ch 1, 5 sc in each of next 2 ch-6 sps; sl st in next sc, 5 sc in next ch-6 sp; sl st in next ch-8 sp on motif, 5 sc in next ch-6 sp] 5 times; sl st in next sc, 5 sc in next ch-6 sp; sl st in next joined ch-8 sps on motifs, 5 sc in each of next 2 ch-6 sps; ch 1, sl st in next ch-8 sp on motif, 5 sc in next ch-6 sp; [sl st in next sc, 5 sc in each of next 2 ch-6 sps; ch 1, sl st in next ch-8 sp on motif, ch 1, 5 sc in each of next 2 ch-6 sps; sl st in next sc, 5 sc in next ch-6 sp; sl st in next ch-8 sp on motif, 5 sc in next ch-6 sp] 5 times; sl st in next sc, 5 sc in next ch-6 sp, sl st in next joined ch-8 sps on motifs, 5 sc in next 2 ch-6 sps; sl st in next ch-8 sp on motif, 5 sc in next ch-6 sp; [sl st in next sc, 5 sc in each of next 2 ch-6 sps; ch 1, sl st in next ch-8 sp on motif, ch 1, 5 sc in each of next 2 ch-6 sps; sl st in next sc, 5 sc in next ch-6 sp; sl st in next ch-8 sp on motif, 5 sc in next ch-6 sp] twice; sl st in next sc, 5 sc in next 2 ch-6 sps; sl st in next ch-8 sp on motif, 5 sc in next 2 ch-6 sps; sl st in next sc, 5 sc in next ch-6 sp; join in first sc.

Finishing

Step 1: On each end of rickrack, sk next tip after last tip worked; cut rickrack between skipped tip and next tip. Apply liquid seam sealant to edge of each cut end. Let dry.

Step 2: On each end, fold rickrack to WS at first tip, then again at next valley to form half-tip. With sewing needle and matching thread, tack fold to WS. Bring half-tip at each end tog to form circle and sew seam securely on WS at folded edge.

Outer Border

On unworked edge of rickrack, join A in tip to right of st worked on opposite side in joining of any 2 motifs.

Rnd 1: Ch 1, sc in same tip; ch 2, sk next valley, *[sc in next tip, ch 5, sc in next valley, ch 5] 16 times; sc in next tip, ch 2, sk next valley; rep from * 3 times more; [sc in next tip, ch 5, sc in next valley, ch 5] 16 times; join in first sc.

Rnd 2: Ch 1, sc in same sc; *2 sc in next ch-2 sp; sc in next sc, [4 sc in next ch-5 sp; sl st in next sc, 4 sc in next ch-5 sp; sc in next sc, ch 4, sl st in sc just made—picot made] 15 times; 4 sc in next ch-5 sp, sl st in next sc, 4 sc in next ch-5 sp, sc in next sc, 2 sc in next ch-2 sp; sc in next sc; rep from * 3 times more; 2 sc in next ch-2 sp; sc in next sc, [4 sc in next ch-5 sp; sl st in next sc, 4 sc in next ch-5 sp; sc in next sc, ch 4, sl st in sc just made—picot made] 15 times; 4 sc in next ch-5 sp, sl st in next sc, 4 sc in next ch-5 sp, sc in next sc, 2 sc in next ch-2 sp; join in first sc.

Fasten off and weave in all ends.

Coaster

Center

With C, ch 7; join to form a ring.

Rnd 1 (RS): Ch 1, [sc in ring, ch 6] 5 times; join in first sc.

Rnd 2: Sl st in next 3 chs of next ch-6 sp; ch 3, in same sp work (dc, ch 2, 2 dc); ch 1; *in next ch-6 sp work (2 dc, ch 2, 2 dc), ch 1; rep from * 4 times more; join in 3rd ch of beg ch-3.

Rnd 3: Sl st in next dc and in next ch-2 sp, ch 3 *(counts as a dc on this and following rnds)* in same sp work (dc, ch 3, 2 dc)—beg shell made; *ch 6, sc in next ch-1 sp, ch 6, **shell** *(see Pattern Stitches)* in next ch-2 sp; rep from * 3 times more; ch 3, sc in next ch-6 sp, ch 6; join in 3rd ch of beg ch-3.

Rnd 4: Sl st in next dc and in next ch-3 sp, beg shell in same sp; *ch 4, [sc in next ch-6 sp, ch 4] twice; shell in ch-3 sp of next shell; rep from * 3 times more; ch 4, [sc in next ch-6 sp, ch 4] twice; join in 3rd ch of beg ch-3. Fasten off.

Outer Edging

Note: *Outer Edging is worked on RS.*

Join C in first tip about 2 inches from end of rickrack.

Rnd 1: Ch 1, sc in same tip; *ch 6, sc in next valley, ch 6, sc in next tip; rep from * 15 times more; join in first sc. Fasten off.

Note: *Cut rickrack about 2 inches from last worked tip.*

Hold RS of center facing RS of border; join C in ch-3 sp of any shell on center.

Rnd 2: Ch 1, sc in same sp; *ch 1, on border, sc in sc on any tip, on center, 3 sc in next ch-4 sp, sc in next ch-4 sp, working through both pieces at same time, sc through same ch-4 sp on center and in sc on next tip on border; on center, sc in same ch-4 sp; 3 sc in next ch-4 sp; on border, sc in sc on next tip, ch 1; on center, sc in ch-3 sp of next shell; rep from * 3 times more; ch 1, on border, sc in sc on any tip, on center, 3 sc in next ch-4 sp, sc in next ch-4 sp, working through both pieces at same time, sc through same ch-4 sp on center and in sc on next tip on border; on center, sc in same ch-4 sp; 3 sc in next ch-4 sp; on border, sc in sc on next tip, ch 1; join in first sc. Fasten off.

Hold piece with RS facing you; join A in any tip.

Rnd 1: Ch 4 *(counts as a dc and a ch-1 sp)*, dc in same tip; *ch 6, sc in next valley, ch 6, in next tip work (dc, ch 1, dc); rep from * 13 times more; ch 6, sc in next valley, ch 6; join in 3rd ch of beg ch-4.

Rnd 2: Ch 1, sc in same ch as joining; *sc in next ch-1 sp, ch 4, sl st in sc just made—picot made; sc in next dc, 6 sc in next ch-6 sp; sl st in next sc, 6 sc in next ch-6 sp; sc in next sc; rep from * 13 times more; sc in next ch-1 sp, ch 4, sl st in sc just made—picot made; sc in next dc, 6 sc in next ch-6 sp; sl st in next sc, 6 sc in next ch-6 sp; join in first sc.

Fasten off and weave in all ends.

How to Check Gauge

A correct stitch gauge is very important. Please take the time to work a stitch gauge swatch about 4 x 4 inches. Measure the swatch. If the number of stitches and rows are fewer than indicated under "Gauge" in the pattern, your hook is too large. Try another swatch with a smaller size hook. If the number of stitches and rows are more than indicated under "Gauge" in the pattern, your hook is too small. Try another swatch with a larger size hook.

Abbreviations & Symbols

beg	begin/beginning
bpdc	back post double crochet
bpsc	back post single crochet
bptr	back post treble crochet
CC	contrasting color
ch	chain stitch
ch-	refers to chain or space previously made (i.e. ch-1 space)
ch sp	chain space
cl	cluster
cm	centimeter(s)
dc	double crochet
dc dec	double crochet 2 or more stitches together, as indicated
dec	decrease/decreases/decreasing
dtr	double treble crochet
fpdc	front post double crochet
fpsc	front post single crochet
fptr	front post treble crochet
g	grams
hdc	half double crochet
hdc dec	half double crochet 2 or more stitches together, as indicated
lp(s)	loops(s)
MC	main color
mm	millimeter(s)
oz	ounce(s)
pc	popcorn
rem	remain/remaining
rep	repeat(s)
rnd(s)	round(s)
RS	right side
sc	single crochet
sc dec	single crochet 2 or more stitches together, as indicated
sk	skip
sl st	slip stitch
sp(s)	space(s)
st(s)	stitch(es)
tog	together
tr	treble crochet
trtr	triple treble
WS	wrong side
yd(s)	yard(s)
yo	yarn over

* An asterisk (or double asterisk **) is used to mark the beginning of a portion of instructions to be worked more than once; thus, "rep from * twice more" means after working the instructions once, repeat the instructions following the asterisk twice more (3 times in all).

() Parentheses are used to set off and clarify a group of stitches that are to be worked all into the same space or stitch, such as "in next corner sp work (2 dc, ch 1, 2 dc)."

[] Brackets are used to enclose instructions that should be worked the exact number of times specified immediately following the parentheses, such as "[2 sc in next dc, sc in next dc] twice."

[] Brackets and () parentheses are used to provide additional information to clarify instructions.

Join—join with a sl st unless otherwise specified.

The patterns in this book are written using United States terminology. Terms that have different English equivalents are noted below.

United States	English
single crochet (sc)	double crochet (dc)
double crochet (dc)	treble (tr)
treble crochet (tr)	double treble (dtr)
double treble crochet (dtr)	triple treble (tr tr)
triple treble crochet (trtr)	quadruple treble (q[uad] tr)
skip (sk)	miss
slip stit ch (sl st)	slip stit ch (ss) or single crochet
gauge	tension
yarn over (yo)	yarn over hook (YOH)

Stitch Guide

Chain—ch:
YO, draw through lp on hook.

Single Crochet—sc:
Insert hook in st, yo and draw through, yo and draw through both lps on hook.

Reverse Single Crochet—
Reverse sc:
Work from left to right, insert hook in sp or st indicated (**a**), draw lp through sp or st - 2 lps on hook (**b**); yo and draw through lps on hook.

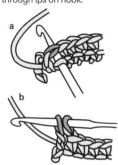

Half Double Crochet—hdc:
yo, insert hook in st, yo, draw through, yo and draw through all 3 lps on hook.

Double Crochet—dc:
yo, insert hook in st, yo, draw through, (yo and draw through 2 lps on hook) twice.

Triple Crochet—trc:
yo twice, insert hook in st, yo, draw through, (yo and draw through 2 lps on hook) 3 times.

Slip Stitch—sl st:
(**a**) **Used for Joinings**
Insert hook in indicated st, yo and draw through st and lp on hook.

(**b**) **Used for Moving Yarn Over**
Insert hook in st, yo draw through st and lp on hook.

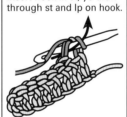

Front Loop—FL:
The front loop is the loop toward you at the top of the stitch.

Back Loop—BL:
The back loop is the loop away from you at the top of the stitch.

Post:
The post is the vertical part of the stitch.

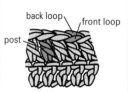

Overcast Stitch is worked loosely to join crochet pieces.

Skill Levels

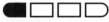

BEGINNER
Beginner projects for first-time crocheters using basic stitches. Minimal shaping.

EASY
Easy projects using basic stitches, repetitive stitch patterns, simple color changes, and simple shaping and finishing.

INTERMEDIATE
Intermediate projects with a variety of stitches, mid-level shaping and finishing.

EXPERIENCED
Experienced projects using advanced techniques and stitches, detailed shaping and refined finishing.

Metric Chart

INCHES INTO MILLIMETERS & CENTIMETERS (Rounded off slightly)

inches	mm	cm	inches	cm	inches	cm	inches	cm
1/8	3		5	12.5	21	53.5	38	96.5
1/4	6		5 1/2	14	22	56	39	99
3/8	10	1	6	15	23	58.5	40	101.5
1/2	13	1.3	7	18	24	61	41	104
5/8	15	1.5	8	20.5	25	63.5	42	106.5
3/4	20	2	9	23	26	66	43	109
7/8	22	2.2	10	25.5	27	68.5	44	112
1	25	2.5	11	28	28	71	45	114.5
1 1/4	32	3.2	12	30.5	29	73.5	46	117
1 1/2	38	3.8	13	33	30	76	47	119.5
1 3/4	45	4.5	14	35.5	31	79	48	122
2	50	5	15	38	32	81.5	49	124.5
2 1/2	65	6.5	16	40.5	33	84	50	127
3	75	7.5	17	43	34	86.5		
3 1/2	90	9	18	46	35	89		
4	100	10	19	48.5	36	91.5		
4 1/2	115	11.5	20	51	37	94		

STEEL THREAD HOOKS METRIC CONVERSION CHART

U.S.	16	14	13	12	11	10	9	8	7	6	5	4	3	2	1	0	00
U.K.	-	7	6½	6	5½	5	4	3	2½	2	1½	1	1/0	2/0	3/0	00	-
Metric-mm	0.6	0.75	0.85	1.00	1.10	1.15	1.25	1.50	1.65	1.80	1.90	2.00	2.10	2.20	2.25	2.50	2.70

We wish to thank Wrights for providing rickrack for this book.

American School of Needlework®
excellence in instruction

DRG Publishing
306 East Parr Road
Berne, IN 46711
©2004 American School of Needlework
TOLL-FREE ORDER LINE or to request a free catalog (800) 582-6643
Customer Service (800) 282-6643, Fax (800) 882-6643

Visit AnniesAttic.com.

Customer Service (800) 282-6643, **fax** (800) 882-6643

We have made every effort to ensure the accuracy and completeness of these instructions. We cannot, however, be responsible for human error, typographical mistakes or variations in individual work.

ISBN:1-59012-106-6   All rights reserved.   Printed in USA   2 3 4 5 6 7 8 9